Updated

Genoa

Travel Guide 2023

The Ultimate Handbook to Explore Italy's Coastal Wonders, From Rich History and Culture to Must See Attractions with Insider Tips for an Authentic Italian Experience

Alec James

Copyright © 2023 by Alec James

Table of Contents

GENOA TRAVEL
Itinerary Planner

Day 1

Time	Activities

Time	Activities

Day 2

Why i Fell In Love With Genoa

Oh, let me take you back to my first visit to the enchanting city of Genoa! I arrived in Genoa late at night, and I was immediately struck by how beautiful the city was. The old town is perched on a hill overlooking the Mediterranean Sea, and the views are simply stunning. I couldn't wait to explore!

The next day, I started my day with a visit to the Aquarium of Genoa. It's one of the largest aquariums in Europe, and it's home to over 10,000 marine animals from all over the world. I spent hours wandering around the aquarium, and I was amazed by all the different creatures I saw.

After the aquarium, I headed to the Old Town. I spent the afternoon wandering around the narrow streets, admiring the architecture, and stopping for coffee and gelato. I also visited the Doge's Palace, which is a beautiful example of Gothic architecture.

In the evening, I had dinner at a traditional Ligurian restaurant. I had the pesto pasta, which was delicious! After dinner, I went for a walk along the waterfront and watched the sunset over the Mediterranean Sea.

Of course, no trip to Genoa would be complete without a visit to Porto Antico. The vibrant colors of the buildings against the backdrop of the deep blue sea created a picture-perfect scene. I spent hours walking along the harbor, admiring the sleek boats and soaking in the maritime atmosphere.

One of the most memorable moments was my encounter with Genoa's culinary delights. I had the pleasure of enjoying trofie al pesto, a dish so simple yet bursting with flavor that I couldn't help but savor every bite. And oh, the gelato – it was as if a tiny scoop of heaven had been served on a cone!

But perhaps my favorite experience was exploring the Palazzi dei Rolli. These opulent palaces, once reserved for the city's noble families, were like something out of a dream. Each room told a different tale of grandeur and history, and I found myself lost in the stories that echoed through those halls.

And then, there was Boccadasse – a charming fishing village that stole my heart. The colorful houses nestled against the cliffs, the sound of waves lapping against the shore, and the sense of tranquility were a balm for my soul. I spent hours simply sitting on the rocky beach, watching the world go by.

I can still remember vividly the party and fun I had in Porto Antico, the Old Port is a great place to party in Genoa. There are a number of bars and clubs located in the area, and the views of the harbor are amazing.

As I left Genoa, a sense of nostalgia lingered. The city had woven its magic around me, leaving me with memories I'll forever cherish.

I had an amazing time in Genoa, and I would definitely recommend it to anyone who is planning a trip to Italy. So, my friend, if you're about to embark on your first journey to Genoa, get ready for an adventure that will fill your heart and soul with the essence of Italy. Explore, savor, and let the city's magic wash over you – and may your experience be as unforgettable as mine.

CHAPTER ONE

INTRODUCTION

Genoa is a port city in northwestern Italy, on the Gulf of Genoa. It is the capital of the Liguria region and also known as the sixth-largest city in Italy. Genoa has a long and rich history, dating back to the 6th century BC. The city was once one of the most powerful maritime republics in the Mediterranean, and it played a major role in the Crusades and the Renaissance.

Genoa is home to a number of important historical and cultural attractions, including the Old Port, the Palazzo Reale, Via Garibaldi, the Cattedrale di San Lorenzo, and the Cimitero Monumentale di Staglieno. The city is also known for its delicious food, its vibrant nightlife, and its stunning views of the Mediterranean Sea.

Genoa is a popular tourist destination, and it is easy to see why. The city has something to offer everyone, from history lovers to foodies to nature lovers. If you are looking for a vibrant and exciting city with a rich history, then Genoa is the perfect place for you.

Getting Acquainted With Genoa

I'm so excited to share with you why you absolutely need to visit Genoa. Trust me, this hidden gem of a city is a treasure trove of experiences just waiting to be uncovered.

History: First things first, the history! Genoa has a long and rich history, dating back to the 6th century BC. The city was once one of the most powerful maritime republics in the Mediterranean, and it played a major role in the Crusades and the Renaissance. There are many historical attractions in Genoa, including the Old Port, the Palazzo Reale,

Via Garibaldi, and the Cattedrale di San Lorenzo. Can you believe that Genoa is the birthplace of none other than Christopher Columbus? Yep, that's right! It's like walking in the footsteps of a legendary explorer. The city's ancient port is brimming with stories and adventures from its maritime past, and you can almost feel the sense of wonder that once inspired those brave voyages.

Once you set foot in the heart of Genoa's Old Town (Centro Storico), you'll be captivated by its narrow cobblestone streets and charming squares like Piazza de Ferrari. I remember strolling through these alleys, feeling like I had stepped back in time. The Doge's Palace is a must-visit – it's an architectural marvel that will leave you in awe.

Now, let's talk about the Acquario di Genova. Oh boy, this place blew my mind! It's one of the largest aquariums in Europe, and believe me, you won't be disappointed. From the colorful marine life to interactive exhibits, it's an enchanting experience for all ages. I couldn't help but feel like a wide-eyed kid again.

Oh, and let's not forget the Lanterna di Genova, that historic lighthouse standing tall and proud. Climb to the top, and you'll be rewarded with breathtaking views of the city and the sparkling Ligurian Sea. It's an Instagram-worthy spot, for sure!

Culture: Genoa is a cultural city with a vibrant arts scene. There are many museums, art galleries, and theaters in Genoa, as well as a number of festivals and events throughout the year. I especially recommend checking out the Galata Museo del Mare, which is one of the largest maritime museums in the world. Genoa is a haven for art and culture enthusiasts too. I was opportuned to catch a captivating performance at Teatro Carlo Felice that left me mesmerized.

Food: Now, let's talk about the food – and trust me, your taste buds will thank you for this trip. Ligurian cuisine is a culinary delight. I still dream about the mouthwatering focaccia, freshly drizzled with olive oil and sprinkled with sea salt. And oh, the pesto! Genoa is the birthplace of pesto sauce, and you won't find it better anywhere else. The local restaurants serve up these delights with love, and it's an experience that will leave you craving for more. The city is home to a number of Michelin-starred restaurants, as well as a number of traditional Ligurian eateries. Some of the most popular dishes in Genoa include focaccia, pesto, and farinata. I highly recommend trying focaccia con le cipolle, which is a type of focaccia with onions. It's so good!

Shopping: If you love shopping like I do, you're in for a treat. Genoa has a mix of trendy boutiques and traditional markets where you can find unique souvenirs to take home. I brought back some lovely handmade crafts and artisanal goods that always remind me of this charming city.

Nightlife: Genoa has a vibrant nightlife scene. There are numerous establishments that stay open late into the night, including taverns, clubs and restaurants. I especially recommend checking out the area around Piazza de Ferrari, which is a great place to go for drinks and dancing.

Nature: Genoa is located on the Mediterranean Sea, and there are a number of beautiful beaches and coves within easy reach of the city. There are also a number of parks and gardens in Genoa, which are perfect for a relaxing stroll. I would recommend taking a walk along the waterfront or visiting the

Parco di Nervi, which is a beautiful park with stunning views of the sea.

But wait, there's more! If you're an outdoor enthusiast, Genoa has got you covered. You can take a boat tour along the stunning coastline, explore nearby natural parks, or simply relax on the sandy beaches.

Genoa is also an ideal base for day trips to Cinque Terre, those picturesque villages clinging to the cliffs by the sea. Portofino is another gem – a sophisticated and elegant coastal town that will steal your heart.

As your guide, I can't stress enough how much you'll love Genoa. The city's warmth, culture, and unique experiences are truly unforgettable. So pack your bags, get ready for a journey through history and culture, and be prepared to create memories that will stay with you forever. I promise you won't regret it!

Things to Expect

Get ready for a fantastic adventure because Genoa has so much to offer. Let me give you the inside scoop on what to expect in this vibrant city.

First things first, Genoa is an absolute stunner. As soon as you arrive, you'll be greeted by the picturesque coastline and the bustling port. The city's rich history as a maritime powerhouse is evident in its stunning architecture and charming old streets. I couldn't help but get lost in the labyrinth of cobblestone alleys in the Old Town – it's like stepping into a time capsule.

One thing you'll notice right away is the friendliness of the locals. Genoese people are warm, welcoming, and proud of their city, and they love sharing its secrets with visitors. Don't hesitate to strike up a conversation – you might end up with some hidden gems and tips that only a local would know.

As you explore the city, you'll come across jaw-dropping landmarks like the Piazza de Ferrari. This bustling square is the heart of Genoa and a great place to soak in the lively atmosphere. The Doge's Palace nearby is a must-see – a glimpse into the city's noble past and a visual feast of frescoes and grand halls.

Now, let's talk about the Acquario di Genova. I'll be honest, I'm a bit of an aquarium enthusiast, and this place blew me away! It's massive and filled with marine wonders from all corners of the globe. It's not just for kids – I felt like a kid myself, completely mesmerized by the underwater world.

One thing I loved about Genoa is how it balances urban charm with nature's beauty. You can take a boat tour along the stunning coastline and see the city from a different perspective. And if you're into hiking, there are nearby natural parks with breathtaking trails that will leave you in awe.

Genoa's nightlife is pretty happening too. The city comes alive after dark, with plenty of bars and clubs to keep you entertained until the wee hours. I found myself dancing the night away, making new friends from all over the world.

In a nutshell, expect to fall in love with Genoa's history, its people, and its culinary delights. Get ready for an adventure that will leave you with unforgettable memories and a heart full of joy. I can't wait for you to experience this beautiful city, my friend. You will have a blast!

10 Must - Know Facts

Most of the things listed here have already been mentioned previously but, i just want to list a few more and to enable you to remember easily without feeling overwhelmed.

1. Genoa is the capital of the Liguria region in northwestern Italy. It is the sixth-largest city in Italy, and it is located on the Gulf of Genoa, which is part of the Mediterranean Sea.

2. Genoa has a long and rich history, dating back to the 6th century BC. The city was once one of the most powerful maritime republics in the Mediterranean, and it played a major role in the Crusades and the Renaissance.

3. Genoa is home to a number of important historical and cultural attractions, including the Old Port, the Palazzo Reale, Via Garibaldi, the

Cattedrale di San Lorenzo, and the Cimitero Monumentale di Staglieno. The city is also known for its delicious food, its vibrant nightlife, and its stunning views of the Mediterranean Sea.

4. Genoa is a relatively affordable city to visit. Accommodation, food, and transportation are all relatively inexpensive compared to other major European cities.

5. Genoa is a great place to visit year-round. The weather is mild in spring, summer, and fall, and there are a number of festivals and events held throughout the year.

6. Genoa is a very walkable city. The historic center is compact and easy to navigate, and there are a number of pedestrian-only streets.

7. Genoa is the birthplace of Christopher Columbus. The famous explorer was born in Genoa in 1451.

8. Local Customs. Genoa has a strong cultural identity, and it's appreciated when visitors respect local customs and traditions. Learning a few basic Italian phrases will also go a long way in connecting with the locals.

9. Genoa is the birthplace of pesto. The classic Ligurian sauce is said to have originated in Genoa in the 19th century.

10. Genoa is a UNESCO World Heritage Site. The historic center of Genoa was designated a World Heritage Site in 2006.

GENOA TRAVEL
Itinerary Planner

	Time	Activities
Day 3		

	Time	Activities
Day 4		

CHAPTER TWO

GETTING TO GENOA

There are a few different ways to get to Genoa, depending on where you're coming from. Whether you're flying, taking a train, or hitting the road, the excitement builds as you get closer to this enchanting city. Let me guide you through getting there like a seasoned traveller.

By Air, Major Airports and Airlines

If you're flying in, Genoa has its own airport – Genoa Cristoforo Colombo Airport (GOA). The airport is located about 6 kilometers from the city center, and there are a number of transportation options available to get you into the city, including buses, taxis, and the Metro. I remember my excitement as the plane descended, offering me a glimpse of the sparkling Mediterranean Sea. From the airport, you can easily reach the city center by taking any of the transportation I mentioned earlier. It's quick and hassle-free, so you'll be sipping an espresso in a charming café in no time!

There are direct flights to Genoa from many major European cities, including Paris and Rome. Travelers from other European cities may need to make a stopover on their journey.. There are direct flights to Genoa from London, Manchester, and Edinburgh. Flights from other UK cities may require a layover. There are no direct flights from the USA to Genoa. However, you can fly to Milan or Rome and then connect to a flight to Genoa.

Getting Flight Tickets

There are many ways to get flight tickets to Genoa from different parts of the world. Here are some of the top choices:

1. Online travel agencies (OTAs): OTAs like Expedia, Kayak, and Skyscanner allow you to compare flights from different airlines and book tickets online.

2. Airline websites: You can also book tickets directly from airline websites. This can sometimes be cheaper than booking through an OTA.

3. Low-cost carriers: Low-cost carriers like Ryanair and EasyJet offer flights to Genoa from a number of European cities. These flights can be very affordable, but they often have restrictions on baggage and other services.

4. Charter flights: Charter flights are often used by groups of people who are traveling together. They can be a good option if you are looking for a specific flight time or date.

Here are some tips for getting cheap flight tickets to Genoa:

- **Book your tickets in advance:** Flights to Genoa can be in high demand, so it is a good idea to book your tickets in advance, especially if you are traveling during the peak season.

- **Be flexible with your travel dates:** If you are flexible with your travel dates, you may be able to find cheap flights.

- **Consider flying into a nearby airport:** If you are on a budget, you might want to consider flying into a nearby airport, such as Milan or Turin. There are a number of transportation options available to get you to Genoa from these airports.

- **Use a price comparison website:** A price comparison website can help you compare flights from different airlines and find the best deal.

By Train, Central Train Stations

Now, if you prefer a scenic ride, traveling by train is a fantastic option. Genoa is well-connected to major Italian cities, so you can easily catch a train from Milan, Florence, or Rome. Trust me; I took the train from Milan, and the journey was seamless, passing through the picturesque Italian countryside. When you arrive at Genoa's main train station, Genova Piazza Principe, you'll be right in the heart of the city, ready to begin your adventure. There are also a number of regional train stations located in the suburbs of Genoa.

There are many ways to get train tickets to Genoa. Here are some of the most used means:

1. Online travel agencies (OTAs): OTAs like Trainline, Omio, and 12Go allow you to compare train tickets from different companies and book tickets online.

2. Train company websites: You can also book tickets directly from train company websites. This can sometimes be cheaper than booking through an OTA.

3. Low-cost carriers: Low-cost carriers like Italo and FlixTrain offer train services to Genoa from a number of cities in Italy. These services can be very affordable, but they often have restrictions on baggage and other services.

4. Trenitalia: This is the Italian national railway company. It's the go-to for anyone looking to travel around the country by train. They offer a wide range of train services, including high-speed trains, regional trains, and night trains.

By Car, Driving to Genoa

If you're driving to Genoa, you'll need to take the A10 autostrada. The autostrada connects Genoa to Milan and Turin, and it is also the main route to the French Riviera. I must admit, driving along the winding coastal roads is therapeutic. Just remember to check the traffic conditions and parking options.

It is possible to drive to Genoa from the UK, but it is a long journey. You will need to take the Eurotunnel to France and then drive down the A10 autostrada to Genoa. It is also possible to drive to Genoa from the USA, but it is a very long journey. You will need to take a ferry from New York or Miami to Italy and then drive down the A10 autostrada to Genoa.

I've personally found that the best way to get to Genoa is by plane. The flights are usually pretty affordable, and it's a quick and easy way to get to the city. Once you're in Genoa, you can use the Metro or buses to get around.

Visa and Entry Requirements

Let's talk about the nitty-gritty of getting into the enchanting city of Genoa. You know, visas and entry requirements – the stuff that ensures you're greeted with a warm "Benvenuti a Genova!" (Welcome to Genoa!) when you arrive.

1. Schengen Zone Magic: If you're an EU citizen or a traveler from one of the Schengen Agreement countries, you're in luck! You won't need a visa to enter Genoa. Just grab your passport or national ID card, hop on a plane, and get ready for an Italian adventure.

2. Non-Schengen Explorers: Now, if you're from a non-Schengen country (like the US, Canada, Australia, New Zealand, most countries in south America and many others), you can stay in Italy – and Genoa – for up to 90 days within a 180-day period for tourism, business, or family visits without a visa. Just ensure your passport is valid for at least three months beyond your intended departure date.

3. Extend Your Stay: Falling head over heels for Genoa and want to stay a bit longer? Well, there's good news! You might be able to apply for a temporary stay permit once you're in Italy. Just remember to check the specific requirements and deadlines.

4. A Piece of Advice: When entering Genoa (or anywhere, really), make sure you have all the necessary documents ready. That means your passport, any required visas, a return ticket, and proof of sufficient funds for your stay. It's like having your travel insurance – a safety net that lets you fully enjoy your adventure.

5. Double-Check, Triple-Check: Entry requirements can change, my friend, so always double-check the most up-to-date information before you travel. Websites of Italian embassies or consulates are your best buddies for this.

6. Friendly Border Control: Genoa is known for its friendly atmosphere, and border control is no exception. Just answer their questions honestly and with a smile – they're there to ensure everyone has a smooth journey.

So, there you have it – the lowdown on visas and entry to the vibrant streets of Genoa. Whether you're in the Schengen zone or not, the city is ready to welcome you with open arms, historical charm, and that irresistible Italian flair.

CHAPTER THREE

WHERE TO STAY

As you plan your trip, you will be on the hunt for the perfect place to stay in Genoa. There are a number of great places to stay in Genoa, depending on your budget and what you're looking for. I've got some fantastic recommendations that will make your stay unforgettable!

Best Areas To Stay

There are a number of great areas to stay in Genoa, depending on your budget and what you're looking for. These are some of my top picks:

1. The Old Town: This is the historical heart of Genoa, and it's home to a number of important attractions, including the Doge's Palace, the Cathedral of San Lorenzo, and the Aquarium of

Genoa. It's also a great place to wander around and explore the narrow streets and alleyways.

2. Porto Antico: This is the old port of Genoa, and it's been transformed into a lively tourist area with shops, restaurants, and bars. There's also a number of historical attractions in the area, such as the Galata Museo del Mare, which is one of the largest maritime museums in the world.

3. Brignole: This is a trendy neighbourhood with a number of bars, restaurants, and shops. It's also home to the University of Genoa, so there's a vibrant student population.

4. Nervi: This is a charming seaside neighborhood with beautiful beaches and stunning views of the Mediterranean Sea. It's a wonderful spot for unwinding and enjoying the outdoors.

Here are some additional tips that I would give to a friend who is planning a trip to Genoa:

- Book your stay in advance: Genoa is a popular tourist destination, so it's a good idea to book your stay in advance, especially if you're travelling during the peak season.
- Avoid the city centre during rush hour: The city centre can be very crowded during rush hour, so if you can, try to avoid travelling during this time.
- Walk along the waterfront: The waterfront is a great place to relax and enjoy the views of the Mediterranean Sea.

Luxury Living

If you're in the mood for a lavish experience, look no further than the luxury hotels in Genoa. Picture yourself in a historical palace turned into a five-star hotel, with elegant rooms, top-notch amenities, and impeccable service. Trust me; you'll feel like royalty! The best part? Some of these hotels are right in the heart of the city, so you'll have easy access to all the major attractions.

Here are some luxury hotels in Genoa, their various prices and location:

1. Palazzo Tursi: This 5-star hotel is located in the heart of the Old Town, and it offers stunning views of the Old Port. The service is excellent, and the rooms are large and luxurious. Prices start at around €200 per night.

2. Hotel Bristol: This 4-star hotel is located in a quiet neighborhood just a short walk from the city center. The rooms are comfortable and stylish, and the breakfast buffet is delicious. Prices start at around €150 per night.

3. NH Collection Genova Marina: This 4-star hotel is located in the Porto Antico area, and it offers stunning views of the harbor. The rooms are modern and stylish, and the hotel has a rooftop terrace with amazing views. Prices start at around €120 per night.

4. Meliá Genova: This 4-star hotel is located in the city center, and it is a short walk from many of the city's most popular attractions. The rooms are spacious and comfortable, and the hotel has a rooftop terrace with views of the city. Prices start at around €100 per night.

5. Starhotels President: This 4-star hotel is located in the city center, and it is a short walk from the train station and the Aquarium of Genoa. The rooms are modern and stylish, and the hotel has a spa and a fitness center. Prices start at around €80 per night.

Charming Boutique Stays

Now, if you want something with a touch of personality and charm, boutique hotels are the way to go. I stayed in one of these gems during my trip, and it was an absolute delight. Think stylish decor, intimate settings, and personalized attention from the staff. You'll feel right at home, and the unique ambiance will add a special touch to your Genoa experience.

Here are some boutique hotels in Genoa, their various prices and location:

1. Hotel Stella Maris: This hotel is located in the Nervi district, and it is housed in a beautiful Art Nouveau building. The rooms are spacious and elegant, and the hotel has a great garden. Prices start at $250 per night. It is close to the Nervi beaches and the Villa Grimaldi park.

2. Hotel Astoria: This hotel is located in the heart of the city center, and it is housed in a historic building. The rooms are stylish and comfortable, and the hotel has a great rooftop terrace. Prices start at $200 per night. It is close to the Doge's Palace, the Aquarium of Genoa, and the Galata Museo del Mare.

3. Hotel Boston: This hotel is located in the Brignole district, and it is housed in a modern building. The accommodations are chic and cozy, and the hotel has an awesome bar and eatery. Prices start at $150 per night. It is close to the Brignole train station and the University of Genoa.

4. Hotel Moderno: This hotel is located in the city center, and it is housed in a restored 19th-century building. The accommodations are chic and cozy, and the hotel has an awesome bar and eatery. Prices start at $125 per night. It is close to the Piazza de Ferrari and the Via XX Settembre shopping street.

5. Hotel Continentale: This hotel is located in the city center, and it is housed in a historic building. The rooms are spacious and elegant, and the hotel has a great bar and restaurant. Prices start at $175 per night. It is close to the Piazza de Ferrari and the Via XX Settembre shopping street.

6. Hotel Il Porticciolo: This waterfront hotel is located in the Nervi district, and it offers stunning views of the Mediterranean Sea. The rooms are modern and stylish, and the hotel has a great rooftop terrace. Prices start at $200 per night. It is close to the Nervi beaches and the Villa Grimaldi park.

7. Hotel Savona 1907: This boutique hotel is located in the Savona district, and it is housed in a restored 19th-century building. The rooms are stylish and comfortable, and the hotel has a great rooftop terrace. Prices start at $175 per night. It is close to the port of Savona and the beaches of Savona

Budget-Friendly Options

Traveling on a budget? No worries – Genoa has got you covered! There are plenty of cozy guesthouses and budget hotels that offer great value for money. I have a friend who stayed in a lovely family-run B&B and raved about the warm hospitality and homemade breakfast. Plus, staying in a more affordable place gives you a chance to splurge on all the delicious food and souvenirs!

Here are some budget-friendly hotels in Genoa, their various prices and location:

1. B&B Il Campanile: This charming B&B is located in a medieval tower in the Old Town. The rooms are small but cozy, and the views are amazing. Prices start at $100 per night. It is close to the Doge's Palace, the Cathedral of San Lorenzo, and the Piazza de Ferrari.

2. Apartments in the Old Town: If you're looking for a more affordable option, you can rent an apartment in the Old Town. This is a great way to experience the city like a local, and you'll have the freedom to come and go as you please. Prices start at $75 per night.

3. Ostello Bello Genova: This hostel is located in the heart of the city center, and it is a great option for budget travelers. The accommodations are shared, yet they are neat and cozy. In the premises you will find a restaurant and a bar. Prices start at $50 per night. It is close to the Doge's Palace, the Aquarium of Genoa, and the Galata Museo del Mare.

4. Genova Suite Rooms: This hotel is located in the Brignole district, and it is a great option for budget travelers who want a bit more privacy. The rooms are small but comfortable, and the hotel has a great bar and restaurant. Prices start at $75 per night. It is close to the Brignole train station and the University of Genoa.

5. Hotel America: This hotel is located in the Nervi district, and it is a great option for budget travelers who want to be close to the beach. The rooms are small but clean, and the hotel has a great garden. Prices start at $60 per night. It is close to the Nervi beaches and the Villa Grimaldi park.

Here are some budget-friendly B&B hotels in Genoa, their various prices and location:

1. B&B Casa Bottega: This B&B is located in a restored 19th-century building in the San Fruttuoso district. The rooms are basic but comfortable, and the breakfast is sumptuous. Prices start at $75 per night. It is close to the Aquarium of Genoa and the Galata Museo del Mare.

2. B&B La Sponda: This B&B is located in a quiet neighborhood just a short walk from the Old Town. The rooms are simple but comfortable, and the breakfast is generous. Prices start at $60 per night. It is close to the Brignole train station and the University of Genoa.

3. B&B Il Moro: This B&B is located in the Nervi district, and it is housed in a beautiful Art Nouveau building. The rooms aren't that big but it's cozy, and the breakfast is delicious. Prices start at $80 per night. It is close to the Nervi beaches and the Villa Grimaldi park.

4. B&B Il Giardino Segreto: This B&B is located in a quiet neighborhood just a short walk from the city center. The rooms are also basic but comfortable, and the breakfast is scrumptious. Prices start at $50 per night. It is close to the Piazza de Ferrari and the Via XX Settembre shopping street.

Mid-Range Comfort

Now, if you're looking for the perfect balance between comfort and affordability, the mid-range hotels in Genoa are just what you need. These places offer comfortable rooms, modern amenities, and a central location without breaking the bank. I opted for one of these during one of my trips, and it was a fantastic decision – convenient, cozy, and just the right price!

The Old Town Experience: For an authentic Genoa experience, consider staying in the heart of the Old Town (Centro Storico). There are charming guesthouses and boutique hotels tucked away in the historic alleys, offering a true taste of Genoese life. You'll wake up to the aroma of freshly baked focaccia and be just steps away from iconic landmarks and local hotspots.

Seaside Retreats

Love the idea of waking up to the sound of the sea? Genoa has some fantastic seaside hotels that offer stunning views of the Ligurian coast. Imagine sipping your morning coffee on a balcony overlooking the azure waters – it's the perfect way to start your day in paradise!

Here are some seaside accommodations in Genoa, their various prices and location:

1. Hotel Villa del Parco: This 4-star hotel is located in the Nervi district, and it offers stunning views of the Mediterranean Sea. The rooms are spacious and elegant, and the hotel has a great garden and swimming pool. Prices start at \\$250 per night. It is close to the Nervi beaches and the Villa Grimaldi park.

2. Hotel Acquaverde: This 4-star hotel is located in the Nervi district, and it is right on the beach. The rooms are modern and stylish, and the hotel has a great rooftop terrace with views of the sea. Prices start at $200 per night. It is close to the Nervi beaches and the Villa Grimaldi park.

3. Hotel Cezanne: This 3-star hotel is located in the Nervi district, and it is a short walk from the beach. The rooms are comfortable and stylish, and the hotel has a great bar and restaurant. Prices start at $150 per night. It is close to the Nervi beaches and the Villa Grimaldi park.

4. Hotel Miramare: This 3-star hotel is located in the Quarto dei Mille district, and it is right on the beach. The rooms are comfortable and stylish, and the hotel has a great rooftop terrace with views of the sea. Prices start at $125 per night. It is close to the Quarto dei Mille beaches and the Galata Museo del Mare.

5. Hotel Bristol Palace: This 4-star hotel is located in the Sampierdarena district, and it is a short walk from the beach. The rooms are spacious and elegant, and the hotel has a great spa and wellness center. Prices start at $225 per night. It is close to the Sampierdarena beaches and the port of Genoa.

Airbnb Gems

Last but not least, consider exploring Airbnb options in Genoa. From cozy apartments to quirky lofts, you'll find a plethora of unique stays that suit your style and budget. It's also an excellent way to connect with locals and get insider tips on the best places to eat and explore.

CHAPTER FOUR

MUST-VISIT ATTRACTIONS

Get ready for a whirlwind tour of the must-visit attractions in Genoa. I'm so excited to share these gems with you – they made my trip truly unforgettable, and I know they'll leave you in awe too!

Genoa Old Town (Centro Storico)

Let's start with the heart and soul of the city – the Genoa Old Town. This place is like a magical maze, with narrow cobblestone streets, charming squares, and historic buildings. I felt like I was wandering through a storybook! Piazza de Ferrari is a focal point, and you'll be captivated by the grandeur of the Doge's Palace (Palazzo Ducale) nearby. Make sure to explore every nook and cranny – there's always something fascinating waiting to be discovered.

Acquario di Genova (Genoa Aquarium)

Oh, my friend, let me tell you about the Acquario di Genova – it's an absolute must-visit! This place completely blew my mind, and I'm sure you'll be just as mesmerized.

Imagine stepping into a massive underwater wonderland filled with the most incredible marine life you can imagine. From majestic sharks gracefully gliding through the water to playful dolphins putting on a show, the Acquario di Genova is a true aquatic paradise.

The best part is that it's not just a regular aquarium – it's one of the largest and most impressive in all of Europe, so you can anticipate a completely engrossing experience. I felt like a kid again, filled with awe and wonder as I explored each exhibit.

One of my favorite parts was the Bigo Panoramic Lift. Imagine being lifted up above the aquarium in a glass sphere, giving you a bird's-eye view of the entire place. It's like you're floating above the sea, surrounded by marine life on all sides – a surreal experience!

And let's not forget about the dolphin and sea lion shows. I was absolutely captivated by their acrobatics and playful antics. It's such a joy to watch these intelligent creatures interact with their trainers and showcase their incredible abilities.

The variety of marine life on display is truly astounding. From colorful tropical fish to majestic rays and enormous sea turtles, every tank is a visual delight. The themed exhibits also give you a glimpse into different aquatic environments, from the Amazon rainforest to the Arctic regions.

I spent hours exploring, but it didn't feel like enough – there's so much to see and experience. And guess what? The Acquario di Genova is not just a place for kids; it's an adventure for everyone, regardless of age. So, don't hold back – dive right in!

My friend, you're in for an unforgettable experience at the Acquario di Genova. Make sure to bring your camera to capture the magical moments, and prepare to be amazed by the beauty and wonder of the underwater world. Trust me; this place will leave a lasting impression on your heart.

Lanterna di Genova (Genoa Lighthouse)

Ah, the Lanterna di Genova – a true beacon of history and beauty in Genoa! Let me share my enchanting experience with this iconic lighthouse.

As soon as I caught sight of the Lanterna, I knew it was going to be something special. It's impossible to miss – standing tall and proud, overlooking the city and the glistening waters of the Ligurian Sea. Trust me, my friend, it's a sight that will leave you in awe.

The lighthouse has a fascinating history that dates back to ancient times. Can you believe it's one of the oldest lighthouses in the world? Imagine the stories it could tell, guiding sailors and ships through centuries of maritime adventures.

Climbing to the top of the Lanterna was an adventure in itself. As I ascended the spiral staircase, my anticipation grew, knowing that breathtaking views awaited me. And boy, was I right! When I reached the top, I was greeted with a panoramic vista that took my breath away. The city's charming rooftops spread out below, and the sea stretched as far as the eye could see. It's a perfect spot to capture some incredible photos and soak in the beauty of Genoa from above.

But let me tell you a little secret – the Lanterna is not just about the view. It's also a symbol of resilience. Throughout history, it has withstood the test of time, surviving wars and natural disasters. It stands tall, a testament to the strength and spirit of the Genoese people.

During my visit, I couldn't help but feel a sense of connection to the city's past as I gazed out from the lighthouse's vantage point. It was a moment of reflection, imagining the sailors and adventurers who had once set sail from this very port.

The Lanterna di Genova is a must-visit, my friend. It's a glimpse into Genoa's maritime legacy and a chance to see the city from a whole new perspective. I recommend visiting during the golden hour when the sun casts a warm glow on the city – it's pure magic!

So, don't pass up on this incredible experience. The Lanterna di Genova will leave an indelible mark on your heart, just like it did on mine. Get ready to embrace the history, the views, and the sheer beauty of this legendary lighthouse. Happy climbing!

Palazzi dei Rolli (Rolli Palaces)

Let me take you on a journey through the magnificent Palazzi dei Rolli, a true treasure trove of history and grandeur in Genoa!

The Palazzi dei Rolli is like stepping into a time machine that transports you back to the glory days of the Genoese nobility. These grand palaces were once the residences of the city's most powerful and influential families during the Renaissance and

Baroque periods. Can you imagine the opulence and sophistication that once graced these halls?

One of the most fascinating things about the Palazzi dei Rolli is their inclusion in the prestigious Rolli di Genova. This was a unique system that assigned a ranking to the palaces, determining which noble families would host important guests like kings and ambassadors. Each year, the families would take turns hosting lavish banquets and events, showcasing their wealth and influence.

As you wander through these architectural marvels, you'll be in awe of the stunning frescoes, intricate stucco work, and elegant courtyards. I remember feeling like I had stepped into a living museum, surrounded by a rich tapestry of history.

One of my favorite palaces is the Palazzo Rosso. Its magnificent façade and ornate interiors left me speechless. The art collection inside is equally impressive, featuring works by renowned Italian artists like Caravaggio, Van Dyck, and Veronese. It's a true feast for art lovers!

Another gem is the Palazzo Bianco, which houses a remarkable collection of European paintings from the 17th to the 18th century. The mix of Italian and Flemish masterpieces is simply captivating.

But the best part about the Palazzi dei Rolli is that you can actually visit some of these palaces. Imagine walking through the same halls that once hosted royalty and dignitaries – it's an experience like no other!

And let me tell you a little secret – visiting these palaces is like embarking on a journey through time. You'll catch glimpses of the past, immerse yourself in the city's rich cultural heritage, and feel a deep connection to Genoa's illustrious history.

So don't miss out on this remarkable experience. The Palazzi dei Rolli will transport you to a bygone era, and you'll be left in awe of the beauty and grandeur that once graced these magnificent palaces. It's a chance to witness history come alive and create memories that will stay with you forever.

Museo di Palazzo Reale

Art enthusiasts, this one's for you! Let me take you on a royal adventure to the Museo di Palazzo Reale – a true gem that will transport you to the opulent world of Genoa's noble past!

Imagine walking through the grand halls of a historic palace, adorned with exquisite artwork and lavish decorations. That's exactly what you'll experience at the Museo di Palazzo Reale. This magnificent museum is a testament to the city's rich cultural heritage and artistic legacy.

As soon as I stepped inside, I was greeted by the majestic beauty of the palace's architecture. The grand staircases, elegant ballrooms, and ornate ceilings took my breath away. I felt like I had entered a fairy tale, surrounded by a world of splendor and luxury.

The museum's art collection is nothing short of extraordinary. You'll be treated to a visual feast of paintings, sculptures, and decorative arts from various periods in history. The works of Italian masters like Titian, Van Dyck, and Veronese grace the walls, showcasing the artistic brilliance of the Renaissance and Baroque eras.

One of the highlights for me was the Sala del Trono (Throne Room). Can you imagine standing in the presence of such regal elegance? I felt like royalty myself, taking in the beauty of the room's intricate details and imagining the grand ceremonies that once took place there.

The museum also offers insights into the daily lives of the Genoese nobility. You'll find rooms that have been preserved in their original state, providing a glimpse into the lifestyle and tastes of the aristocracy. It's like stepping back in time and being a guest in the palace itself.

And let me share a little tip – if you have a passion for history and art, consider joining a guided tour. The knowledgeable guides will take you on a journey through the palace's history and enrich your experience with fascinating stories and anecdotes.

But the best part of the Museo di Palazzo Reale is that it's not just a place for art enthusiasts. It's a journey of discovery and wonder for everyone. Whether you're a history buff or simply appreciate the beauty of fine craftsmanship, this museum will leave you in awe.

So don't miss the chance to immerse yourself in the splendor of the Museo di Palazzo Reale. It's a magical experience that will leave you with a deeper appreciation for Genoa's rich cultural heritage and a sense of connection to the city's illustrious past.

Boccadasse - Fishing Village

Allow me to introduce you to the picturesque fishing village of Boccadasse – a hidden gem that stole my heart and will surely steal yours too!

As you walk along the charming streets of Genoa, you might stumble upon a path that leads you to Boccadasse. It's like going back in time. The moment I arrived, I was captivated by the village's colorful houses that line the tiny harbor. It's like a scene straight out of an Italian movie!

Boccadasse has a unique atmosphere that's hard to describe. It's peaceful, quaint, and oh-so-charming. I felt a sense of tranquility wash over me as I strolled along the seafront, soaking in the beauty of the surroundings.

The harbor is the heart of Boccadasse, and you'll find colorful fishing boats bobbing gently in the water. It's a hub of activity, with local fishermen going about their daily routines. Watching them work and hearing the gentle lapping of the waves against the shore was a moment of pure serenity.

The village is small but has so much character. There are hidden alleys and narrow passages waiting to be explored. I felt like I was on a delightful treasure hunt, uncovering secret spots and finding hidden gems around every corner.

One of the best parts of Boccadasse is the beach. Oh, the beach! It's a haven for relaxation and unwinding. I couldn't resist kicking off my shoes and feeling the soft sand between my toes. It's the perfect spot to bask in the sun, listen to the gentle waves, and enjoy a lazy afternoon with a good book.

And let me tell you, Boccadasse is not just about scenic views and relaxation. It's also a foodie paradise! The village is dotted with charming trattorias and cafes where you can savor some of the freshest seafood you'll ever taste. I remember indulging in a delicious plate of pasta with a view of the sea – it was a moment of culinary bliss!

But what truly makes Boccadasse special is the warmth of the locals. The people here are friendly and welcoming, making you feel like part of the community. I struck up conversations with some of the residents, and they were more than happy to share stories about their beloved village.

So, my friend, don't miss the chance to experience the enchantment of Boccadasse. It's a place where time seems to stand still, and you can embrace the simple joys of life. From the colorful houses to the charming beach and the delightful cuisine, every moment spent in Boccadasse will leave you with cherished memories.

Cattedrale di San Lorenzo

Let me take you on a journey to the Cattedrale di San Lorenzo – a stunning architectural marvel and a spiritual oasis in the heart of Genoa!

As you approach the cathedral, you'll be greeted by its majestic facade, adorned with intricate carvings and sculptures. The Cattedrale di San Lorenzo has a timeless elegance that immediately captivates the eye. I remember being in awe as I stood before the grand entrance, feeling a sense of reverence and wonder.

Stepping inside, I was greeted by a sense of serenity and tranquility. The hushed atmosphere, the soft glow of the stained glass windows, and the gentle scent of incense created a sacred space that invited contemplation and reflection.

The cathedral's interior is adorned with art of history. The vaulted ceilings soar above you, adorned with frescoes that tell stories of faith and devotion. I was mesmerized by the intricate details and the craftsmanship that went into creating this masterpiece.

The highlight of the Cattedrale di San Lorenzo is its majestic dome, which is a marvel of engineering and artistic prowess. As I gazed up at the soaring dome, I couldn't help but feel a sense of awe and wonder at the human ingenuity that brought this magnificent structure to life.

One of the most significant features of the cathedral is the Cappella di San Giovanni Battista (Chapel of St. John the Baptist). This beautifully decorated chapel houses the relics of St. John the Baptist, making it a sacred place of pilgrimage and devotion for believers.

The cathedral also boasts an impressive collection of religious art, including paintings and sculptures from various periods. I spent hours marveling at the works of art, which served as a window into the spiritual and artistic legacy of Genoa.

But what truly touched my heart was the sense of community and devotion within the cathedral. As I attended a service, I witnessed the strong bond between the people and their faith. The singing, the prayers, and the sense of unity were deeply moving, and I felt a connection to something greater than myself.

Don't miss the chance to visit the Cattedrale di San Lorenzo. It's a place of beauty, history, and spirituality that will leave you with a sense of awe and reverence. Whether you're religious or not, this cathedral is a testament to the enduring power of human creativity and faith. Take a moment to embrace the tranquility, immerse yourself in the art and history, and find peace in the sanctuary of the Cattedrale di San Lorenzo.

Doge's Palace (Palazzo Ducale)

Prepare to be transported back in time as we step into the magnificent Doge's Palace – a symbol of power, history, and architectural brilliance in Genoa!

As you approach the Palazzo Ducale, you can't help but be in awe of its grandeur and imposing presence. This majestic palace stands as a testament to the city's rich history and the seat of power during the days of the Republic of Genoa.

Stepping inside, I felt like I was entering a living museum. The grand courtyards, opulent halls, and splendid staircases take you on a journey through the centuries. You can almost feel the weight of history on your shoulders as you walk through the same halls that once housed Genoa's rulers and government officials.

One of the highlights of the Doge's Palace is the Sala del Maggior Consiglio (Hall of the Grand Council). It's an immense space adorned with stunning frescoes, depicting the glory and triumphs of the Republic of Genoa. I remember standing there, gazing up at the artwork, and feeling a sense of pride for the city's illustrious past.

The palace is also home to a treasure trove of art, with paintings and sculptures that tell stories of political intrigue, heroic deeds, and the city's maritime heritage. I found myself getting lost in the details of the artworks, each one a window into a different era of Genoa's history.

But the most iconic feature of the Doge's Palace is the Scala dei Giganti (Staircase of the Giants). As you ascend this majestic staircase, you can't help but feel a sense of reverence for the past and the giants who once walked these steps.

What struck me the most during my visit was the sense of power and prestige that the palace exudes. It's a place where decisions that shaped the destiny of Genoa were made, and standing there, I couldn't help but imagine the voices that once echoed through these halls.

The Doge's Palace is not just a monument to the past; it's a living reminder of the city's resilience and enduring spirit. It's a chance to step into the shoes of the city's rulers, to immerse yourself in the history and culture that shaped Genoa.

Don't miss the opportunity to visit the Doge's Palace. It's a journey through time, a chance to connect with the city's heritage, and an experience that will leave you in awe of the magnificence of Genoa's past. Embrace the history, marvel at the art, and let the grandeur of the Palazzo Ducale take your breath away.

Here are other few must-visit attractions in Genoa:

● **The Port of Genoa:** This is the oldest port in the Mediterranean Sea, and it's still an important commercial port today. You can take a boat tour of the port, or you can just wander around and watch the ships come and go.

● **The Nervi district:** This is a seaside district with beautiful beaches and stunning views of the Mediterranean Sea. There are also a number of gardens and parks in the area, making it a great place to relax and enjoy the outdoors.

● **The Galata Museo del Mare:** This is a maritime museum that tells the story of Genoa's seafaring history. The museum is housed in a former warehouse, and it has a number of interactive exhibits that make it a great place to learn about the history of the sea.

CHAPTER FIVE

THINGS TO DO IN GENOA

Apart from visiting the top attractions in Genoa, there are lots of other things to do as well. Get ready for an unforgettable adventure in Genoa, with these fantastic things to do, your days will be filled with wonder, history, flavors, and delightful surprises. Let me be your guide to all the fantastic things to do in this incredible city. From exploring historical gems to indulging in mouthwatering treats, Genoa has it all!

Cultural Experiences

Let's talk about the incredible cultural experiences that await you in Genoa. This city is bursting with art, history, and traditions that will leave you with a profound appreciation for its rich cultural heritage.

1. Art Galleries and Museums: If you're an art enthusiast like me, you're in for a treat! Genoa boasts some fantastic art galleries and museums that house masterpieces from various periods. The Galleria Nazionale di Palazzo Spinola is a personal favorite – the exquisite paintings and decorative arts took my breath away! And don't miss the Museo d'Arte Orientale Edoardo Chiossone, a hidden gem that houses an incredible collection of Asian art. Trust me; you'll be amazed by the diversity of cultural influences.

Other museums worth checking out includes;
● **Museo d'Arte Contemporanea di Villa Croce:** For contemporary art enthusiasts, this museum is a must-visit. Housed in the picturesque Villa Croce, the museum showcases a diverse range of contemporary artworks from Italian and international artists. The ever-changing exhibitions

will keep you coming back for more artistic inspiration.

• **Museo d'Arte Sacra di Sant'Agostino:** Step into the world of religious art at the Museo d'Arte Sacra di Sant'Agostino (Museum of Sacred Art of St. Augustine). This intimate museum showcases a beautiful collection of religious artifacts, including paintings, sculptures, and liturgical objects. It's a serene and contemplative space, perfect for reflecting on the spiritual aspect of Genoa's culture.

Be prepared to be captivated by the art galleries and museums of Genoa. From classic masterpieces to contemporary creations, the art scene in Genoa is as diverse as the city itself.

2. Festivals and Events: Let's dive into the vibrant world of festivals and events in Genoa. Throughout the year, this lively city comes alive with

celebrations that showcase its rich culture, traditions, and the warmth of its people. So, grab your calendar and get ready to mark these dates for an unforgettable time in Genoa!

- **Festa della Madonna della Guardia (Last Sunday in May):** This is one of the most beloved festivals in Genoa, and it's close to my heart too. On the last Sunday of May, the city gathers to honor the Madonna della Guardia, the patron saint of Genoa. The festivities include a solemn procession, where a statue of the Madonna is carried through the streets, followed by lively celebrations, concerts, and fireworks. It's a beautiful blend of spirituality and joyous merrymaking that brings the whole community together.

- **Genoa International Boat Show (Late September to Early October):** Ah, the sea is in the city's soul, and this event celebrates Genoa's maritime spirit in all its glory! The Genoa International Boat Show, held at the historic Porto Antico, is a nautical paradise. You'll find everything from luxurious yachts to cutting-edge marine technology. Whether you're a boating enthusiast or not, it's an event that will leave you in awe of the wonders of the sea.

- **Genoa Science Festival (October):** Calling all curious minds! The Genoa Science Festival is a captivating event that brings science and innovation to the forefront. With a wide range of interactive exhibitions, workshops, and talks, it's a great opportunity to explore the latest discoveries and embrace your inner scientist. I had a blast at the festival, diving into the fascinating world of technology and discoveries.

- **Genoa Pesto World Championship (April/May):** Are you a foodie like me? Then, this event is a must-attend! The Genoa Pesto World Championship celebrates the city's most famous culinary delight – pesto! Prepare for a culinary showdown as participants compete to create the most delicious pesto sauce. You'll also get a chance to savor the mouthwatering results and learn some secrets of the perfect pesto recipe. It's a true taste of Genoa's gastronomic heritage.

- **Euroflora (April/May, every five years):** This extraordinary event takes place once every five years and transforms the city's stunning parks into floral wonderlands. Euroflora is a botanical dream, with intricate flower arrangements, themed gardens, and a burst of colors. It's like stepping into a magical garden straight out of a fairy tale.

- **Notte Bianca (September):** Get ready for a night of pure fun and excitement! Notte Bianca (White Night) is a city-wide celebration that lasts until the wee hours of the morning. The streets come alive with concerts, performances, and art installations. It's a night to let loose, embrace the city's vibrant energy, and create unforgettable memories.

• **Luci d'Artista:** This is a light festival that takes place in December. There are light installations all over the city, creating a magical atmosphere.

• **Carnevale di Genova:** This is a lively carnival that takes place in February. There are parades, street parties, and costume contests.

• **International Book Fair of Genoa:** This is a major book fair that takes place in October. There are book signings, readings, and lectures by authors from all over the world.

So as you plan your visit to Genoa, make sure to coincide it with one of these fantastic festivals and events. Each celebration offers a unique glimpse into the heart and soul of the city. From religious traditions to maritime wonders, scientific discoveries, and cultural delights, Genoa's events calendar has something for everyone.

3. Theatres and Performing Arts: Prepare to be mesmerized by the city's vibrant cultural scene, where talent and creativity take center stage. From classic operas to modern plays, Genoa has something to offer for every performing arts enthusiast like you and me. So, grab your tickets and get ready for a theatrical adventure!

Here are a few of the theaters and performing arts venues that I recommend checking out:

- **Teatro Carlo Felice:** This is the main opera house in Genoa. It's a beautiful building with a rich history, and it hosts a variety of performances, from opera to ballet to classical music concerts.

- **Teatro Gustavo Modena:** This is a smaller theater that's known for its innovative productions. It hosts a variety of performances, from plays to musicals to dance performances.

- **Piccolo Teatro di Genova:** This is a contemporary theater that's known for its experimental productions. It hosts a variety of performances, from plays to musicals to dance performances.

- **Teatro Akropolis:** This is a venue for experimental and alternative theater. It hosts a variety of performances, from plays to musicals to dance performances.

- **Auditorium RAI:** This is a large auditorium that's used for a variety of performances, including concerts, operas, and plays.

I've seen a few performances at the Teatro Carlo Felice, and I've always been impressed with the quality of the productions. The acoustics are amazing, and the stage is huge. I also really like the Piccolo Teatro di Genova. They always put on interesting and thought-provoking productions.

If you're interested in theater and performing arts, I highly recommend checking out what's happening in Genoa. Check the schedules of the theaters and venues before you go. Some of the theaters and venues have specific seasons, so it's important to check and see what's on during your visit. Be prepared to be wowed. The theater and performing arts scene in Genoa is world-class, so be prepared to be wowed by the quality of the productions.

4. Traditional Music and Dance: Don't miss the chance to experience traditional Genoese music and dance. Wander through the streets, and you might come across a group of musicians playing lively tunes on the accordion or the mandolin. It's infectious – you won't be able to resist tapping your feet!

Genoa has a rich musical history, and there are a number of traditional genres that are still performed today. Some of the most popular include:

● **Canzone genovese:** This is a type of folk song that is typically accompanied by a guitar or mandolin. The lyrics are often about love, loss, or the sea.

● **Tarantella genovese:** This is a type of folk dance that is characterized by its fast tempo and energetic movements. It is said to have originated in the city of Genoa, and it is often performed during festivals and celebrations.

- **Ballo liscio:** This is a type of ballroom dance that is popular in Italy. It is characterized by its intriguing and smooth, flowing moves.

- **Pizzicato:** This is a type of folk music that is characterized by its pizzicato (plucked) strings. It is often performed in the countryside, and it is said to have originated in the region of Liguria.

I've had the opportunity to see a few traditional music and dance performances in Genoa, and I've always been impressed by the energy and passion of the performers. The music is beautiful, and the dancing is mesmerizing.

7. **The Sense of Community:** One thing that struck me during my time in Genoa was the strong sense of community and pride in their heritage. The locals are warm and welcoming, and they're always eager to share stories about their city and traditions. Engage with the people, strike up a conversation, and you'll find that connecting with the locals is a cultural experience in itself.

Get ready to immerse yourself in the cultural tapestry of Genoa. From art and opera to music, dance, and delectable cuisine, this city has so much to offer. Embrace the cultural experiences, let your curiosity guide you, and create memories that will stay with you forever.

Enjoying Culinary Delights

Let's talk about one of the most delightful aspects of Genoa – its incredible culinary scene. Get ready to embark on a mouthwatering adventure as we explore the flavors that will leave you craving for more! Ligurian cuisine is a Mediterranean cuisine that is characterized by its fresh, simple ingredients. The region is home to a long coastline, so seafood is a major component of the cuisine. Other popular ingredients include olive oil, tomatoes, basil, and pesto.

1. Local Dishes to Try:

Genoa is a port city, so seafood is a big part of the cuisine. Some of the most popular dishes include:

- **Pesto, Pesto, Pesto:** Oh, where do I even begin? Genoa is the birthplace of the famous basil-based sauce, and let me tell you, it's a game-changer! When I had my first taste of authentic pesto in Genoa, I was blown away by the fresh, vibrant flavors. You have to try it with some handmade trofie pasta – a match made in culinary heaven!

- **Focaccia**: Brace yourself for some serious carb heaven! Genoa's focaccia is unlike any other you've tasted. It's soft, pillowy, and topped with just the right amount of olive oil and salt. Whether you prefer the classic version or one with cheese or onions, each bite is a little piece of heaven.

- **Seafood Extravaganza:** Being a coastal city, Genoa knows how to do seafood right! From succulent grilled fish to mouthwatering seafood risotto, you'll be in seafood paradise. I remember savoring a plate of seafood spaghetti while overlooking the sparkling Ligurian Sea – an experience I'll never forget.

- **Farinata – A Unique Delight:** Here's a little secret not many know about – try farinata! It's a savory pancake made from chickpea flour, olive oil, and a touch of rosemary. It's simple yet bursting with flavor. I enjoyed it as a snack, and it was the perfect treat to satisfy my cravings.

- **Pansoti:** These are stuffed pasta pockets that are typically filled with a mixture of spinach, ricotta cheese, and herbs. They're then served with a walnut sauce.

- **Gelato Galore:** You can't leave Genoa without indulging in some gelato. Trust me; it's a taste of pure happiness! The gelaterias here take pride in their artisanal gelato, and you'll find flavors that are unique to the city. Pistachio, hazelnut, and fruity sorbets – you'll be spoilt for choice!

- **Focaccia di Recco:** You might think we already covered focaccia, but there's more! Focaccia di Recco is a special kind of focaccia filled with ooey-gooey stracchino cheese. The combination of the crispy dough and the creamy cheese is simply divine. It's a must-try while you're in Genoa.

- **Ciuppin:** This is a fish soup that is made with a variety of different types of seafood, including clams, mussels, and sardines. This soup is a great choice for a cold day; it's full of flavor and sure to fill you up.

- **Local Markets and Trattorias:** Want to explore Genoa's culinary delights like a local? Head to the local markets like Mercato Orientale and Mercato di Via XX Settembre. There, you'll find fresh produce, artisanal cheeses, and a variety of local specialties. And when it comes to trattorias, let me tell you, you're in for a treat. The cozy, family-run eateries serve up homemade dishes that are full of love and flavor.

Ligurian cuisine is also known for its desserts, which are often made with local ingredients like lemons, chestnuts, and honey. Some popular desserts include:

- **Pandolce:** This is a traditional Genoese cake that is made with dried fruits, nuts, and spices. It is typically served during the holidays.

- **Biscotti di Prato:** These are crunchy almond biscuits that are typically dipped in Vin Santo, a sweet wine.

- **Cassata:** This is a layered cake that is made with sponge cake, ricotta cheese, chocolate, and candied fruit. It is typically served during the holidays.

If you are looking for a delicious and authentic Mediterranean cuisine, then Ligurian cuisine is a great option. The region is home to a variety of fresh, simple ingredients that are used to create flavorful and satisfying dishes.

I've had the opportunity to try all of these dishes, and they're all delicious. My personal favorites are pesto and focaccia. I love the way the basil in the pesto tastes with the pasta, and the focaccia is always so fresh and flavorful.

2. Popular Restaurants and Eateries:

If you're a foodie, I highly recommend checking out the culinary scene in Genoa. There are a number of great restaurants serving traditional Genoese cuisine, as well as more modern restaurants that are putting a creative spin on classic dishes.

Here are a few of my favorite restaurants in Genoa:

- **Trattoria Il Panino:** This is a great place to try traditional Genoese cuisine. They have a wide variety of pasta dishes, as well as some great seafood dishes. They are located in the Old Town, and their price range is around €15-€30 per person.

- **Trattoria Aurora:** This restaurant is another great place to try traditional Genoese cuisine. They have a cozy atmosphere and the food is always delicious. They are located in the Old Town, and their price range is around €15-€30 per person.

- **Nino:** This restaurant is a bit more upscale, but the food is absolutely amazing. They have a tasting menu that changes seasonally, and it's a great way to try a variety of different dishes. They are located in the Old Town, and their price range is around €40-€60 per person.

- **Il Genovese:** it's a great place to try modern takes on classic Genoese dishes. The meal is usually great and the chef is quite creative. They are located in the Old Town, and their price range is around €30-€50 per person.

- **La Sponda:** it's a Michelin-starred restaurant that serves seafood dishes. They have a beautiful view of the harbor, and the food is simply outstanding. They are located in the Old Town, and their price range is around €60-€100 per person.

- **Baretto:** it's a great place to go for drinks and snacks. They have a wide variety of cocktails, and their food menu is full of delicious small plates. They are located in the Old Town, and their price range is around €10-€20 per person.

- **Giacomo Bistrot:** it's a great place to go for lunch or dinner. They have a variety of pasta dishes, as well as some great pizzas. They are located in the Old Town, and their price range is around €15-€30 per person.

• **Trattoria Il Moro:** This is a great place to go for traditional Genoese seafood dishes. They have been in business for over 100 years, and the food is always delicious. They are located in the Old Town, and their price range is around €20-€40 per person.

Shopping in Genoa

Shopping in Genoa is an absolute delight! Get ready to explore a mix of modern boutiques, local markets, and charming shops that cater to all your shopping desires. Here's a guide to make the most of your shopping experience in this beautiful city:

Shopping Districts and Streets:

1. Via XX Settembre: Let's start with the heart of Genoa's shopping scene. Via XX Settembre is a bustling street lined with shops, boutiques, and department stores. You'll find a wide variety of fashion brands, trendy accessories, and stylish shoes. It's the perfect place to update your wardrobe and find unique pieces to take home as souvenirs.

2. Mercato Orientale: For an authentic local shopping experience, head to Mercato Orientale. This vibrant market is a feast for the senses, with stalls selling fresh produce, local cheeses, cured meats, and more. It's a great place to stock up on ingredients for a picnic or pick up some delicious Italian treats.

3. Antiques and Artisanal Crafts: If you're a fan of antiques and artisanal crafts, Genoa won't disappoint. Explore the narrow streets of the Old Town, and you'll stumble upon charming shops selling unique handmade jewelry, ceramics, and artworks. Don't be afraid to haggle a little – you might score a one-of-a-kind treasure!

4. Luxury Shopping at Galleria Mazzini: If luxury shopping is more your style, Galleria Mazzini is the place to be. This elegant shopping arcade is home to high-end fashion brands, jewelry stores, and luxury boutiques. Even if you're not shopping, it's worth a visit just to admire the beautiful architecture.

5. Focaccerie and Specialty Food Shops: Don't forget to bring home some edible souvenirs! Genoa's focaccerie offer an array of freshly baked focaccia and other savory treats. And don't miss the specialty food shops, where you can find authentic Ligurian olive oil, pasta, pesto, and other regional delicacies to take home.

6. La Casana dei Mercanti: For a unique shopping experience, visit La Casana dei Mercanti, a collective of local artisans and designers. Here, you'll find handcrafted goods, including clothing, accessories, and home decor items, all made with love and creativity.

7. Porto Antico: When you're done shopping, take a stroll at Porto Antico – the old port area. It's a vibrant hub with a mix of shops, restaurants, and entertainment venues. You can shop for souvenirs, enjoy the sea breeze, and even catch a glimpse of the famous Bolla (the Biosphere) designed by Renzo Piano.

Traditional Markets

The traditional markets in Genoa are a true reflection of the city's vibrant and authentic spirit. Get ready to immerse yourself in the lively atmosphere and discover a treasure trove of fresh produce, local specialties, and unique finds. Let me take you on a tour of some of the most charming traditional markets in Genoa:

1. Mercato Orientale: As I mentioned earlier, Mercato Orientale is a must-visit for an authentic local experience. This bustling market has been a gathering place for Genoese locals for over a century. You'll find a colorful array of fruits, vegetables, cheese, cured meats, and seafood. The aroma of fresh herbs and spices fills the air, making it a delight for food enthusiasts.

2. Mercato di Via XX Settembre: Located on Via XX Settembre, this market offers a mix of local produce, specialty foods, and artisanal products. It's a great place to stock up on fresh ingredients for a picnic or indulge in some delectable Italian treats. Don't forget to try some Ligurian olives and sun-dried tomatoes – they are simply divine!

3. Mercato della Foce: This market is a hidden gem tucked away in the Foce neighborhood. It's a favorite among locals for its relaxed and friendly atmosphere. You'll find a variety of stalls selling everything from clothing and accessories to fresh produce and household items. It's a great place to browse and discover some unique finds.

4. Mercato delle Erbe: Step into the historic Mercato delle Erbe, and you'll be transported back in time. This indoor market has been around since the early 1900s and still retains its charming old-world charm. Here, you can shop for fresh fruits, vegetables, meat, and fish, as well as artisanal products and flowers.

5. Mercato di Piazza Sarzano: This market is a lively spot in the heart of the Old Town. It's known for its fresh produce, but you'll also find vendors selling clothing, accessories, and household items. It's a great place to soak in the local ambiance and discover some hidden gems.

6. Mercatino di Piazza Fontane Marose: If you're looking for antiques and vintage items, head to Piazza Fontane Marose on the third Saturday of every month. The Mercatino (flea market) is a treasure trove of unique finds, from old books and records to vintage clothing and home decor.

Each traditional market has its own unique charm and offers a glimpse into the daily life and culture of the city. Whether you're shopping for fresh ingredients or hunting for one-of-a-kind treasures, the markets of Genoa will leave you with lasting memories and a deeper appreciation for the city's authenticity.

Unique Souvenirs to Buy

The joy of bringing back unique souvenirs from your travels! Genoa has a plethora of charming and authentic keepsakes to choose from. Here are some special souvenirs that will remind you of the city's beauty and warmth:

1. Ligurian Olive Oil: Genoa is surrounded by olive groves, so it's no surprise that the city produces exceptional olive oil. Look for bottles of high-quality, locally produced olive oil to take back home. It's not only delicious but also a healthy reminder of your time in Genoa.

2. Handcrafted Ceramics: Genoa is known for its beautiful ceramics, often featuring intricate designs and bright colors. Look for handcrafted bowls, plates, or tiles that capture the essence of the city's culture and architecture.

3. Ligurian Wines: Raise a toast to your Genoa adventures with a bottle of Ligurian wine. The region produces some delightful wines, including Vermentino and Rossese. Visit a local enoteca (wine shop) or a winery to find the perfect bottle to bring back as a souvenir.

4. Genoa Pesto World Championship Apron: If you're a fan of pesto, you'll love this quirky souvenir. Look for an apron or kitchen towel featuring the Genoa Pesto World Championship logo. It's a fun and practical way to remember your culinary experiences in Genoa.

5. Italian Leather Goods: Italy is renowned for its high-quality leather goods, and Genoa is no exception. Treat yourself to a stylish leather wallet, handbag, or belt as a fashionable and lasting souvenir.

6. Art Prints and Postcards: Take home a piece of Genoa's artistic heritage with art prints or postcards featuring famous landmarks and local artwork. They make for beautiful wall decor and heartfelt gifts.

7. Lanterna di Genova: This is the iconic lighthouse of Genoa. You can find souvenirs with the Lanterna's image all over the city.

As you explore the charming streets of Genoa, keep an eye out for these unique souvenirs. Each one captures a slice of the city's culture and will bring a smile to your face as you reminisce about your unforgettable time in Genoa.

Outdoor Activities

Genoa is not just a city of art and culture; it also offers a range of exciting outdoor activities that allow you to immerse yourself in the beauty of nature and the sparkling Mediterranean Sea. Here are some outdoor activities that will make your time in Genoa even more memorable:

1. Explore the Old Town on Foot: The best way to soak in the city's charm is by exploring the Old Town on foot. Wander through the narrow alleys, discover hidden squares, and marvel at the stunning architecture. Don't forget to visit the famous Piazza De Ferrari and the charming Via Garibaldi, both UNESCO World Heritage sites.

2. Walk along the Seaside Promenade: Take a leisurely stroll along the seaside promenade (Corso Italia) and enjoy the sea breeze. The promenade offers breathtaking views of the sea and the iconic Lanterna di Genova (Genoa Lighthouse). It's a perfect spot for a relaxing walk or a romantic evening with loved ones.

3. Boat Tours and Cruises: Hop on a boat tour or cruise to explore the coastline and surrounding areas of Genoa. You can choose from short harbor cruises to longer excursions that take you to picturesque coastal towns like Portofino and Cinque Terre.

Boat tours and harbor cruises are fantastic ways to experience the beauty of Genoa from the sparkling waters of the Mediterranean Sea. From breathtaking coastal views to up-close encounters with iconic landmarks, these tours offer unforgettable experiences. Here are some boat tours and harbor cruises you can enjoy in Genoa:

- **Harbor Cruise of Porto Antico:** Start your maritime adventure by taking a harbor cruise around Porto Antico, the historic old port of Genoa. From the water, you'll have a unique perspective of the city's skyline, including the iconic Lanterna di Genova (Genoa Lighthouse) and the Biosphere designed by Renzo Piano. It's a great way to see the city's bustling waterfront and the mix of modern and historic architecture.

• **Genoa to Portofino Cruise:** Embark on a scenic cruise from Genoa to the picturesque fishing village of Portofino. This coastal journey offers breathtaking views of rugged cliffs, lush greenery, and crystal-clear waters. Once in Portofino, you'll have time to explore the charming village, enjoy some local seafood, and take in the idyllic scenery.

• **Genoa to Cinque Terre Cruise:** For a more extended coastal adventure, consider a cruise from Genoa to the enchanting Cinque Terre. This UNESCO World Heritage Site is known for its five colorful cliffside villages, and the cruise allows you to admire the dramatic coastline and unique architecture of these charming towns.

- **Whale Watching Tours:** If you're a nature enthusiast, you'll love the opportunity to embark on a whale watching tour from Genoa. The Ligurian Sea is home to various marine species, including dolphins, whales, and sea turtles. With an experienced guide, you'll have a chance to witness these majestic creatures in their natural habitat.

- **Sunset Sailing Tours:** Treat yourself to a romantic sunset sailing tour along the Genoa coastline. As the sun dips below the horizon, the sky transforms into a canvas of colors, making for a truly magical experience. Some tours even offer the option to enjoy aperitivo (Italian happy hour) on board, adding to the enchantment of the evening.

- **Mini Cruises and Day Trips:** If you're short on time, consider a mini cruise or a day trip along the Ligurian coast. These tours offer a taste of the sea and the surrounding beauty without committing to a full-day journey.

4. Visit the Natural Parks: Genoa is surrounded by beautiful natural parks that offer hiking trails and stunning vistas. Head to Parco Naturale Regionale del Beigua or Parco di Villa Durazzo Pallavicini for a day of outdoor adventure and tranquility.

Here are some of the best natural parks to explore in Genoa:

● **Parco delle Mura:** This park is located on the hills surrounding Genoa. It's an awesome spot to take a hike or go for a bike ride. You can also visit the ruins of the old city walls.

● **Parco Naturale Regionale dell'Aveto:** This park is located in the mountains north of Genoa. It's a great place to go for hiking, camping, and fishing.

- **Parco Naturale Regionale di Portofino:** This park is located on the coast south of Genoa. It's a great place to go for hiking, swimming, and sunbathing.

- **Parco del Beigua:** This park is located in the hills between Genoa and Savona. It's a great place to go for hiking, biking, and rock climbing.

5. Biking and Cycling: If you enjoy cycling, rent a bike and explore the city and its surroundings on two wheels. There are bike paths along the coast and through the parks, providing a scenic and eco-friendly way to get around.

6. Beaches and Water Sports: Genoa's coastline is dotted with beautiful beaches where you can soak up the sun and enjoy a refreshing swim. Some beaches also offer water sports activities like kayaking, paddleboarding, and snorkeling.

Genoa is blessed with some beautiful beaches along its stunning coastline. Whether you're looking for sandy stretches to relax on or rocky coves to explore, the city and its surrounding areas offer a variety of beach experiences. Here are some of the best beaches in and around Genoa:

• **Boccadasse Beach:** One of the most iconic and picturesque beaches in Genoa is Boccadasse. This charming fishing village is just a short distance from the city center and offers a small pebble beach nestled between colorful houses. It's a perfect spot to relax, enjoy the sea breeze, and soak in the local ambiance.

• **Spiaggia di Nervi:** Located in the neighborhood of Nervi, this sandy beach is popular among both locals and tourists. The beach is easily accessible and offers clear waters for swimming. Nearby, you'll find the beautiful Nervi Park, perfect for a leisurely stroll after a day on the sand.

- **Punta Vagno:** For a more secluded beach experience, head to Punta Vagno. This rocky cove is surrounded by lush greenery and offers a peaceful setting for sunbathing and swimming. It will make a great escape from the city's hustle and bustle.

- **Paraggi Beach:** Although a short drive from Genoa, Paraggi Beach is well worth the visit. Located near the picturesque village of Portofino, this beach is renowned for its crystal-clear waters and scenic surroundings. It's a paradise for those who like snorkeling and diving.

- **Arenzano Beach:** Just west of Genoa, the town of Arenzano boasts a long sandy beach that's perfect for families and sunbathers. The calm waters make it a great spot for swimming and water sports, and the beach is lined with restaurants and cafes for a delightful seaside meal.

- **Varazze Beach:** A little further west of Genoa, you'll find Varazze Beach, a wide sandy stretch popular among both locals and visitors. It's an excellent spot for beach sports and beachfront relaxation, with numerous beach clubs offering amenities.

- **Celle Ligure Beach:** If you're up for a short drive east of Genoa, Celle Ligure Beach awaits you with its golden sands and inviting waters. The beach is well-equipped with facilities and offers a lively atmosphere, especially during the summer months.

7. Picnicking at Parco di Nervi: Pack a picnic and head to Parco di Nervi, a picturesque park with lush greenery and stunning sea views. It's a perfect spot to relax, read a book, or have a delightful outdoor meal with friends and family.

8. Rock Climbing at Monte Reixa: If you're an adventurous soul, head to Monte Reixa for some rock climbing. The rugged cliffs offer exciting challenges for climbers of all levels, and the views from the top are absolutely rewarding.

9. Golfing: Enjoy a round of golf at one of Genoa's golf courses, such as the beautiful Circolo Golf e Tennis Rapallo, which offers stunning views of the surrounding hills and the sea.

I've had the opportunity to try some of these activities, and I've loved them all. My personal favorites are hiking and cycling. I love the feeling of being outdoors and exploring the city from a different perspective.

Enjoying Nightlife (Party and Fun)

The nightlife in Genoa is as vibrant as the city itself! When the sun sets, the city comes alive with a plethora of entertainment options to suit every taste. Whether you prefer to dance the night away, enjoy live music, or relax with a drink in hand, Genoa has something for everyone. Here's a guide to enjoying the nightlife in this lively city:

1. Bars and Pubs

• **Baretto:** This is a popular bar in the Old Town that is known for its cocktails. It's a great place to go for a drink before or after dinner.

• **Giacomo Bistrot:** This is a great place to go for a casual meal and a drink. They have a wide variety of beers on tap, and the food is delicious.

• **Trattoria Il Panino:** This is a traditional Genoese restaurant that also has a great bar. They have a wide variety of wines and liquors, and the food is excellent.

- **Trattoria Aurora:** This is another great traditional Genoese restaurant that has a great bar. They have a wide variety of wines and liquors, and the food is excellent.

- **Covo di Nord Est:** This is a legendary club in Genoa that has been open since 1986. It's a great place to go for electronic music and dancing.

2. Nightclubs and Dancing Venues

- **Superga:** This is a rooftop bar with stunning views of the city. It's a great place to go for a drink before or after dinner.

- **Qualude RockClub:** This is a popular nightclub that is known for its rock music. It's an awesome spot to go and have a blast while dancing.

- **La Claque:** This is a small club that is known for its live music. It's an awesome spot to check out new and upcoming bands.

- **Il Molo:** This is a large club that is known for its electronic music. It's a great place to go to dance and party.

- **Magazzini Generali:** This is a former warehouse that has been converted into a large club. It's a great place to go to see big name DJs and artists.

3. Live Music and Performances

- **Teatro Carlo Felice:** This is the main opera house in Genoa. They host a variety of performances throughout the year, including opera, ballet, and concerts.

- **Teatro Politeama Genovese:** This is another large theater in Genoa. They put on a range of shows throughout the year, such as plays, musicals, and concerts.

- **Auditorium Fabrizio De André:** This is a smaller theater in Genoa that is known for its intimate atmosphere. They host a variety of performances throughout the year, including plays, concerts, and stand-up comedy.

- **Casa del Jazz:** This is a jazz club in Genoa that hosts a variety of performances throughout the year.

- **Bohème Caffè Concerti:** This is a cafe in Genoa that hosts a variety of live music performances throughout the year.

Here are other nightlife activities you can enjoy in Genoa

• **Piazza delle Erbe and Piazza delle Vigne:** These lively squares in the heart of the Old Town are popular meeting spots for locals and visitors alike. Here, you'll find numerous bars and cafes with outdoor seating, creating a vibrant atmosphere. It's a great place to grab a drink, people-watch, and soak in the lively ambiance.

• **Porto Antico:** The waterfront area of Porto Antico transforms into a bustling nightlife hub after dark. From stylish cocktail bars to trendy nightclubs, you'll find a variety of venues to enjoy. The area around Piazza delle Feste is particularly known for its nightlife scene.

•. **Via di Sottoripa:** This lively street is home to many wine bars and taverns, making it a perfect spot for an evening of wine tasting and socializing. Try some local wines and indulge in a traditional aperitivo, where drinks are often served with complimentary snacks.

- **Teatro Carlo Felice:** For a more refined and cultural night out, consider attending a performance at Teatro Carlo Felice, the city's renowned opera house. Enjoy an opera, ballet, or classical music concert in a stunning historic setting.

- **Moonlit Seaside Stroll:** If you prefer a quieter evening, take a moonlit stroll along the seaside promenade. The city's coastal views take on a magical glow under the moonlight, creating a romantic and serene atmosphere.

Day Trips and Excursions

One of the best things about Genoa is its strategic location, making it a perfect base for exciting day trips to some incredible destinations nearby. Let me be your travel buddy and share some of my favorite day trip experiences from Genoa:

1. Cinque Terre – A Colorful Coastal Gem: First on the list has to be Cinque Terre – a collection of five charming coastal villages that will steal your heart. I hopped on a train from Genoa to Riomaggiore and spent the day exploring the colorful houses, picturesque harbors, and stunning cliffside trails. Each village has its unique charm, and I couldn't resist taking a refreshing dip in the crystal-clear waters. Oh, and the seafood there is to die for!

2. Portofino – A Glamorous Escape: For a taste of luxury and glamour, I took a boat ride from Genoa to the chic harbor town of Portofino. As the boat approached the coastline, I was greeted by the sight of opulent yachts and pastel-colored buildings nestled against lush green hills. I explored the narrow streets, indulged in some retail therapy at high-end boutiques, and enjoyed a seafood feast with a breathtaking view of the harbor.

3. Camogli – The Charm of Simplicity: Camogli, oh Camogli! This charming fishing village captured my heart with its simplicity and authentic Italian vibes. I took a short train ride from Genoa and was welcomed by a picturesque harbor lined with colorful houses and fishing boats. The pebble beach was a perfect spot to unwind and savor some gelato while gazing at the serene sea views. The best part? Camogli is a hidden gem, less crowded than other tourist spots.

4. Santa Margherita Ligure – Beauty in Abundance:
Another gem within easy reach from Genoa is Santa Margherita Ligure. It's a coastal town that exudes elegance and charm. I spent the day exploring the

stunning villas, lush gardens, and vibrant town center. The lively promenade is lined with cozy cafes and gelaterias – the perfect places to sit back and people-watch.

5. San Fruttuoso – A Hidden Cove with a Secret Abbey: San Fruttuoso is like a well-kept secret tucked between rocky cliffs. I took a boat ride from Camogli to this hidden cove and was amazed by its beauty. The medieval abbey nestled on the shore adds an air of mystery to the place. I enjoyed swimming in the turquoise waters and snorkeling to explore marine life.

6. Rapallo: This is a town located on the coast of Liguria. It's a popular tourist destination, and it's known for its beautiful beaches, its lively nightlife, and its medieval old town.

CHAPTER SIX

PRACTICAL INFORMATION

Now that you're all set to explore Genoa, let me share some practical information to make your trip smooth and enjoyable. From transportation tips to local customs, here's everything you need to know:

Getting Around

Genoa has an efficient public transportation system that includes buses and a metro. I found the buses to be a convenient way to get around the city, and they also serve some nearby attractions. Don't forget to grab a Genoa Welcome Card for unlimited public transport and discounts on attractions.

Navigating Genoa is a breeze, thanks to its efficient public transportation system and pedestrian-friendly layout. Let me break down the different modes of transportation to help you get around the city with ease:

1. Buses: Genoa's bus network is extensive and covers most areas of the city, making it a convenient way to get around. Look for bus stops with yellow signs displaying the route numbers and schedules. You can purchase tickets from tobacco shops, newsstands, or on board the bus. As soon as you board the bus, don't forget to validate your ticket.

2. Metro: Genoa has a metro system that serves the city's urban areas and connects the city center to the outskirts. It's a fast and reliable mode of transportation, especially for longer distances. The metro runs from early morning until late at night, and tickets are the same as for the bus.

The bus and metro systems in Genoa are efficient and affordable. A single ticket costs €1.50 and is valid for 100 minutes of travel on any combination of buses and the metro. You can also buy a day pass for €4.50 or a three-day pass for €12.

3. Funiculars and Elevators: Genoa is a hilly city, and to navigate the steep inclines, you'll find funiculars and elevators at various locations. These charming transport options not only help you get around but also offer scenic views of the city.

4. Walking: Genoa is a city meant to be explored on foot! Many of its attractions are within walking distance of each other, especially in the historic center. Stroll through the narrow streets, and you'll stumble upon hidden gems and beautiful architecture.

5. Cycling: Genoa is a great city to explore on bike. The city has a number of bike lanes and paths that make it easy to get around. Here are some specific bike routes that you can take in Genoa:

- **The Waterfront:** This is a great route for a leisurely bike ride. You'll get to enjoy the views of the port and the city skyline.
- **The hills:** If you're looking for a workout, you can take a bike ride up to the hills that surround Genoa. The views from the top are amazing!
- **The Old Town:** This is a more challenging route, but it's worth it to see the narrow streets and the historic buildings.

6. Taxis: Taxis are readily available throughout the city, and you can easily hail one from designated taxi stands or call a taxi service. However, keep in mind that they can be more expensive compared to public transportation. The base fare is €3.50 and the fare increases by €0.25 per kilometer.

7. Renting a Car: If you plan to explore the surrounding areas or go on day trips, you might consider renting a car. However, keep in mind that navigating the narrow streets and finding parking can be challenging in the city center. Here are some driving tips in Genoa:

● **Be prepared for narrow streets and one-way traffic:** The streets in Genoa can be very narrow and winding, and there are a lot of one-way streets. Be sure to pay attention to the signs and be prepared to give way to pedestrians and other vehicles.

● **Be aware of the traffic laws:** The traffic laws in Italy are different from the traffic laws in the United States. Be sure to familiarize yourself with the traffic laws before you start driving in Genoa.

- **Don't drink and drive:** The legal limit for blood alcohol content in Italy is 0.05%. If you are caught driving over the limit, you will be arrested and fined.

- **Be prepared for traffic jams:** The traffic in Genoa can be very congested, especially during rush hour. Be prepared to wait in traffic and be patient.

- **Use a sat nav:** If you are not familiar with the streets in Genoa, I would recommend using a sat nav to help you get around. This will help you avoid getting lost and getting into traffic jams.

Language and Communication

One thing to keep in mind if you're planning a trip to Genoa is the language. The official language in Genoa is Italian. However, you will find lots of people in tourist areas who speak English. I've found that most people in Genoa are happy to help tourists, even if they don't speak English fluently.

Here are a few tips for communicating in Genoa:

- **Learn some basic Italian phrases:** This will show the locals that you're making an effort to communicate in their language. Even if you only know a few phrases, it will go a long way.
- **Be patient:** Italians can be slow to speak English, so be patient and don't get frustrated.
- **Use hand gestures:** Italians use a lot of hand gestures when they talk. This can be helpful if you're not sure what someone is saying.
- **Smile and be friendly:** Italians are generally very friendly and welcoming. If you smile and be friendly, they'll be more likely to help you.

Things To Pack

Hey there, my fellow adventurer! As you are ready to embark on your Genoa journey, let's make sure you're packing all the right essentials to make your trip smooth and enjoyable. Here's a rundown of what to bring:

1. Comfortable Walking Shoes: Trust me, you'll want to explore every charming corner of Genoa on foot. Pack comfortable walking shoes that can handle cobblestone streets and hilly terrain. Your feet will thank you!

2. Weather-Appropriate Clothing: Genoa enjoys a Mediterranean climate, so think light and breathable clothes for the warmer months and a mix of layers for cooler times. Oh, and don't forget a swimsuit for beach days!

3. Sunscreen and Hat: The Italian sun can be quite intense, especially during the summer. Pack a good sunscreen and a stylish hat to protect yourself while wandering the city or lounging on the beach.

4. Travel Adapter: Keep your devices charged and ready for all those Instagram-worthy moments. Italy uses Type F plugs, so make sure to bring a travel adapter that works with this socket type.

5. Portable Charger: You'll be snapping photos, checking maps, and maybe even using translation apps. A portable charger will save you from those dreaded low-battery moments.

6. Reusable Water Bottle: Staying hydrated is key, so having a reusable water bottle will save you money and help you reduce single-use plastic waste. Fill up at fountains throughout the city!

7. Crossbody Bag or Backpack: A hands-free bag is a must for exploring. It keeps your belongings secure and allows you to move freely while keeping your essentials close.

8. This travel guide and Map: While I'm here to provide you with all the info you need, having a physical travel guide or a map can be handy for quick references and planning.

9. Phrasebook or Language App: While many locals speak English, a few Italian phrases go a long way in making connections and showing appreciation for the local culture.

10. Medications and First Aid Kit: Bring any prescribed medications you might need, along with a basic first aid kit for those unexpected situations.

11. Camera or Smartphone: Genoa is a picturesque city, and you'll want to capture its beauty. Whether it's a dedicated camera or your trusty smartphone, make sure you have a way to snap those memories.

12. Travel Documents: Keep your passport, ID, travel insurance, and any necessary visas organized and easily accessible.

13. Local Currency: While credit cards are widely accepted, having some local currency (Euros) on hand for small purchases or places that don't accept cards can be handy.

14. Snacks: It's always good to have some snacks on hand for those moments when you're on the go or waiting for transportation.

Remember, my friend, packing light and smart is the key to a stress-free and enjoyable trip. Now that you're equipped with these essentials, you're all set to explore Genoa like a pro.

Safety and Security

Genoa is generally a safe city for travelers, but like any other place, it's essential to take common-sense precautions. Be mindful of your possessions, particularly in busy places, and be conscious of what's going on around you. Here are some Genoa safety tips:

General Safety Tips:

- Always be mindful of your surroundings.
- Avoid carrying valuables, especially at night.
- Pickpockets should be avoided, especially in crowded places.
- If you get lost, seek assistance from a police officer or a local.
- Avoid drinking tap water, stick to bottled water at all times.
- Learn about local customs and traditions. Respect the indigenous culture.

Prevention of Pickpocketing:

- Keep your possessions close to you, especially your wallet, phone, and passport.
- Do not, under any circumstances, leave your backpack on the ground.
- Keep your bag on your lap if you're sitting.
- Keep an eye out for folks who are too close to you.
- If you believe you are being followed, seek refuge in a crowded area or at a police station.

Medical and Health Services:

- There are several hospitals and clinics in Genoa. If you want medical assistance, go to the nearest hospital or clinic. If you want immediate medical attention, you can also call an ambulance.
- In Italy, dial 112 in an emergency. If you have travel insurance, make sure you bring it with you.

Here are some emergency numbers in Genoa:

- Police: 112
- Fire department: 115
- Ambulance: 118
- Coast guard: 1530
- Tourist police: 010 557 7200

It is important to note that these numbers are for emergencies only. If you have a non-emergency, you can call the local tourist information number: 010 557 7200.

Safety doesn't mean being overly cautious – it's about being prepared and making informed decisions. Genoa is a fantastic city to explore, and by following these safety tips, you're ensuring that your adventure is both enjoyable and secure. So, go out there, soak in the beauty, and create wonderful memories in this captivating Italian gem!

Wi-Fi and Connectivity

Wi-Fi and connectivity in Genoa are generally good. There are a number of free Wi-Fi hotspots around the city, including in most cafes, restaurants, libraries, airports and hotels. You can also purchase a prepaid Wi-Fi card from a local retailer.

If you need to stay connected while you're in Genoa, I recommend purchasing a prepaid Wi-Fi card. You can buy these cards at most convenience stores and tobacco shops. They usually come with a certain amount of data that you can use within a certain period of time.

Common Tourist Complaints and Solutions

Here are some common tourist complaints about Genoa and possible solutions:

- **Pickpockets:** Pickpocketing is a common problem in Genoa, especially in crowded areas. To avoid being pickpocketed, be sure to keep your belongings close to you, especially your wallet, phone, and passport. Don't put your bag down on the ground, even for a moment. If you're sitting down, keep your bag on your lap. Take note of people who are standing too close to your position. If you think you're being followed, go to a crowded area or a police station.

Solution: Be aware of your surroundings and take precautions to protect your belongings.

- **Language barrier:** English is not widely spoken in Genoa, so there can be a language barrier between tourists and locals. If you don't speak Italian, it can be difficult to communicate with people. To overcome this, try to learn some basic Italian phrases before you go. You can also use a translation app or dictionary to help you communicate.

Solution: Learn some basic Italian phrases or use a translation app or dictionary to help you communicate.

- **Public transportation:** The public transportation system in Genoa can be confusing and difficult to use. If you're not familiar with the system, it can be easy to get lost or take the wrong bus. To avoid this, make sure you have a map of the city and know where you're going before you start using public transportation.

Solution: Plan your route in advance and make sure you have a map of the city. Ask a local for help if you're not sure where you're going.

- **Rude locals:** Some tourists complain that the locals in Genoa can be rude and unhelpful. This is not always the case, but it is something to put in mind as you are visiting. If you have a negative experience with a local, don't let it ruin your trip. Just move on and try to have a positive experience with someone else.

Solution: Don't let a few bad experiences ruin your trip. Just move on and try to have a positive experience with someone else.

So, my friend, armed with this practical information, you're all set to dive into the beauty and charm of Genoa. Embrace the local culture, try the delicious food, and immerse yourself in the city's rich history. I'm sure you'll fall in love with Genoa, just like I did. Have a fantastic time, and enjoy every moment of your adventure in this captivating Italian gem! Safe travels!

COVID-19 Regulations

I've been to Genoa a few times since the pandemic, and I've found that the COVID-19 regulations are very strict. However, I think it's important to follow the regulations to keep yourself and others safe. As of March 8, 2023, the following are the COVID-19 regulations for entry into Italy:

- **Proof of vaccination:** You must show proof of vaccination to enter most public places, including restaurants, bars, museums, and shops.
- **Face masks:** Face masks are required in all indoor public places, including restaurants, bars, museums, and shops.
- **Social distancing:** You must maintain social distancing of at least 1 meter from other people in all public places.
- **Testing:** You may be required to take a COVID-19 test if you are displaying symptoms of the virus.

- **Children under 6 years of age are exempt from the vaccination and testing requirements:**

Children under 6 years of age do not need to show proof of vaccination or a negative COVID-19 test to enter Italy.

If you are not vaccinated, you may be denied entry to Genoa. You may also be required to quarantine for 5 days upon arrival.

I know that following all of these regulations can be a lot to remember, but it's important to do your part to keep yourself and others safe.

Here are some additional tips for staying safe during your trip to Genoa:

- **Stay up-to-date on the latest COVID-19 regulations:** The regulations can change frequently, so it's important to stay up-to-date on the latest changes. You can find the latest regulations on the website of the Italian government.

- **Be prepared to show proof of vaccination:** You should always be prepared to show proof of vaccination when you enter a public place. You can keep your vaccination card in your phone or in a hard copy.

- **Wear a face mask:** Even if you are vaccinated, you should still wear a face mask in all indoor public places. This will help protect yourself and others from the virus.

- **Avoid crowded places:** If you can, avoid crowded places, especially during peak tourist season. This will help you reduce your risk of exposure to the virus.

- **Wash your hands frequently:** Wash your hands with soap and water for at least 20 seconds, especially after being in a public place. If you don't have access to soap and water, you can also use hand sanitizer.

Useful Apps and Other Resources

Technology is your ally when exploring Genoa. Here are some apps and resources that you might find helpful for your trip to Genoa:

1. Google Maps: Google Maps is a great app for getting around Genoa. It can help you find your way around the city, and it also has information on public transportation and attractions.

2. Citymapper: Citymapper is another great app for getting around Genoa. It's similar to Google Maps, but it has more detailed information on public transportation.

3. TripAdvisor: TripAdvisor is another great resource for planning your trip to Genoa. It has reviews of hotels, restaurants, and attractions.

4. XE Currency Converter: XE Currency Converter is a handy app for converting currencies. This can be helpful when you're budgeting for your trip or when you're shopping in Genoa.

5. Translator: If you don't speak Italian, a translator app can be helpful. This can be helpful when you're interacting with locals or when you're trying to read signs.

With these apps in your pocket, you'll be well-equipped to navigate, discover, and enjoy all that Genoa has to offer. So, load up your devices, embrace the convenience of technology, and get ready to embark on an unforgettable adventure!

GENOA TRAVEL
Itinerary Planner

Day	Time	Activities
Day 5		

Day	Time	Activities
Day 6		

CHAPTER SEVEN

ITALIAN PHRASEBOOK AND SUGGESTED ITINERARY

Ciao, amico mio! Ready to dive into the heart of Genoa armed with a little Italian charm? I've got you covered with a handy Italian phrasebook and a suggested itinerary that'll make your trip unforgettable. Let's get started!

Italian Phrasebook

Learning a few Italian phrases can open doors (literally!) and create wonderful connections with locals. Here are some must-know phrases to sprinkle into your conversations. Let's make sure you're ready to charm the locals and navigate the city with ease:

Greetings and Basic Phrases

- Ciao! (chow) - Hello/Goodbye (casual)

- Buongiorno! (bwon-jor-noh) - Good morning!

- Buonasera! (bwon-ah-seh-rah) - Good evening!

- Per favore. (pehr fah-vo-reh) - Please.

- Grazie. (grahts-ee-eh) - Thank you.

- Prego. (preh-go) - You're welcome.

- Scusa. (skoo-sah) - Sorry.

- Mi dispiace. (mee dee-spee-ah-cheh) - I'm sorry.

- Sì. (see) - Yes.

- No. (noh) - No.

- Non capisco. (non kah-pee-sko) - I don't understand.

Getting Around

- Dove si trova...? (doh-veh see troh-vah) - Where is...?

- Quanto costa? (kwan-toh koh-stah) - How much does it cost?

- A che ora...? (ah keh oh-rah) - At what time...?

- Posso avere...? (pohs-so ah-veh-ray) - Can I have...?

- Mi può aiutare? (mee pwoh ah-yoo-tah-reh) - Can you help me?

- Mi scusi, non parlo italiano molto bene. (mee skoo-zee non par-lo ee-tah-lee-ah-no mohl-toh beh-neh) - Excuse me, I don't speak Italian very well.

- Dove si trova la stazione? (doh-veh see troh-vah lah stah-tsee-yoh-neh) - Where is the train station?

Eating and Drinking

- Un tavolo per uno/due, per favore. (oon tah-vo-lo pehr oo-no/doo-eh, pehr fah-vo-reh) - A table for one/two, please.

- Il menù, per favore. (eel meh-noo, pehr fah-vo-reh) - The menu, please.

- Vorrei... (vor-ray) - I would like...

- Acqua, per favore. (ah-kwah, pehr fah-vo-reh) - Water, please.

- Il conto, per favore. (eel kohn-toh, pehr fah-vo-reh) - The bill, please.

- Posso avere il conto, per favore? (pohs-so ah-veh-ray eel kohn-toh, pehr fah-vo-reh) - Can I have the bill, please?

- Mi piace molto! (mee pee-ah-cheh mohl-toh) - I like it very much!

Directions and Transportation

- Dov'è la fermata dell'autobus? (doh-veh lah fehr-mah-tah dell ow-toh-boos) - Where is the bus stop?

- Dov'è la stazione della metropolitana? (doh-veh lah stah-tsee-yoh-nah dell-ah meh-tro-po-lee-tah-nah) - Where is the metro station?

- Quanto costa un biglietto? (kwan-toh koh-stah oon beel-yet-to) - How much does a ticket cost?

- A che ora parte il treno? (ah keh oh-rah par-teh eel treh-no) - At what time does the train leave?

- Mi può indicare la strada per...? (mee pwoh een-dee-kah-reh lah strah-dah pehr) - Can you show me the way to...?

Emergency Phrases

- Aiuto! (ah-yoo-toh) - Help!

- Chiamate la polizia! (kee-ah-mah-teh lah poh-lee-tsee-ah) - Call the police!

- Chiamate un'ambulanza! (kee-ah-mah-teh oon ahm-boo-lahn-tsah) - Call an ambulance!

- Ho bisogno di aiuto. (oh bee-sohn-yoh dee ah-yoo-toh) - I need help.

- Mi sono perso/a. (mee soh-noh pehr-soh/ah) - I'm lost.

- Ho perso il mio passaporto. (oh pehr-soh eel mee-oh pahs-sah-por-toh) - I've lost my passport.

- Mi hanno rubato il mio portafoglio. (mee ahn-no roo-bah-toh eel mee-oh por-tah-foh-lyoh) - Someone stole my wallet.

- Mi sento male. (mee sehn-toh mah-leh) - I feel sick.

- Dove si trova l'ospedale? (doh-veh see troh-vah lohs-peh-dah-leh) - Where is the hospital?

Now you're armed with the tools to navigate Genoa like a pro! Embrace the language, connect with the locals, and savor every moment of your Italian adventure. Buon viaggio!

Suggested Itineraries

Now, let's sprinkle some Italian flair into your Genoa adventure with a suggested itinerary:

3-Days Itinerary

Day 1: Exploring the Historic Heart

- Start your morning with a cappuccino and cornetto at a local café.
- Stroll through the Old Town (Centro Storico), admiring the medieval architecture.
- Visit the Genoa Cathedral (Cattedrale di San Lorenzo) and soak in its history.
- Enjoy a leisurely lunch at a traditional trattoria – try some local trofie al pesto.

- Explore the narrow alleys of the Caruggi, the charming maze-like streets.
- Visit the Palazzo dei Rolli and marvel at the grandeur of the Renaissance palaces.
- Head to the Porto Antico area for a relaxed dinner with stunning harbor views.

Day 2: Maritime Magic and Artistry

- Begin your day at the Acquario di Genova – dive into the underwater world.
- Walk along the picturesque Boccadasse, a fishing village turned cozy neighborhood.
- Enjoy a seafood lunch overlooking the Ligurian Sea.
- Visit the Palazzo Ducale, exploring the Doge's Palace and its art exhibitions.
- Wind down with a stroll along the Passeggiata Anita Garibaldi, a scenic seaside promenade.
- Treat yourself to a fancy dinner at a waterfront restaurant.

Day 3: Coastal Escapes and Cultural Delights

- Take a day trip to Cinque Terre – hike the trails or hop between the colorful villages.

- Savor some local street food for lunch, perhaps a delicious farinata.

- Return to Genoa and explore the historic Teatro Carlo Felice for some cultural enrichment.

- Indulge in a gelato as you wander the streets one last time.

- Share stories and laughter over a delightful Italian dinner with newfound friends.

7-Days Itinerary

Here's a balanced and exciting plan that allows you to explore the city's highlights, as well as nearby attractions. Feel free to adjust it to your preferences and pace:

Day 1: Arrival and Introduction to Genoa

- Arrive in Genoa and check into your accommodation.

- Start your journey with a leisurely walk along the Passeggiata Anita Garibaldi, enjoying the sea breeze and the beautiful views.

- Explore the historic heart of Genoa, including the Cattedrale di San Lorenzo and the charming streets of the Old Town (Centro Storico).

- Indulge in a traditional Genoese dinner at a local trattoria.

Day 2: Maritime Exploration

- Begin your day at the Acquario di Genova, one of the largest aquariums in Europe.

- Afterward, take a walk along Porto Antico, admiring the impressive architecture and vibrant atmosphere.

- Have a delicious seafood lunch at a waterfront restaurant.

- Visit the Galata Maritime Museum to delve deeper into Genoa's maritime history.

- Spend your evening exploring the picturesque neighborhood of Boccadasse and enjoying a gelato by the sea.

Day 3: Day Trip to Cinque Terre

- Embark on an early morning train journey to Cinque Terre – the charming five coastal villages.

- Hike the breathtaking trails connecting the villages or hop on the train between them.

- Explore the colorful streets, enjoy the stunning views, and savor a seafood-focused lunch.

- Return to Genoa in the evening and relax at a local eatery.

Day 4: Art and History

- Visit the Palazzo Ducale (Doge's Palace) to admire its artistic treasures and exhibitions.

- Wander through the Caruggi (narrow alleyways) of the Old Town, discovering hidden gems and local shops.

- Enjoy a hearty Italian lunch at a cozy trattoria.

- Spend your afternoon at the Genoa Museum of Art (Museo d'Arte Orientale), exploring its unique collection.

- Wrap up the day with a relaxing dinner at a local restaurant.

Day 5: Day Trip to Portofino and Santa Margherita Ligure

- Take a day trip to the charming coastal towns of Portofino and Santa Margherita Ligure.

- Explore the colorful harbor of Portofino and hike to the stunning overlook at Castello Brown.

- Enjoy a seafood lunch in one of the local eateries.

- Head to Santa Margherita Ligure to wander its elegant streets and relax by the sea.

- Return to Genoa in the evening for a delicious dinner.

Day 6: Cultural Delights

- Visit the Royal Palace Museum (Museo di Palazzo Reale), showcasing the history and grandeur of the former royal residence.
- Explore the Palazzi dei Rolli, admiring the architectural splendor of these historic palaces.
- Have a leisurely lunch at a café, savoring local specialties.
- Spend your afternoon exploring the Teatro Carlo Felice or the Galleria Nazionale di Palazzo Spinola for more cultural enrichment.
- Celebrate your last night in Genoa with a special dinner.

Day 7: Farewell and Departure

- Enjoy a leisurely breakfast and take a last stroll through the city's streets.

- Depending on your departure time, you might have a little more time to explore a favorite spot or do some last-minute souvenir shopping.
- Bid farewell to Genoa and head to the airport or train station for your onward journey.

There you have it, my friend – a 7-day adventure that allows you to immerse yourself in Genoa's rich history, stunning architecture, delicious cuisine, and nearby coastal gems. Remember, this is just a guide – feel free to adjust it to your interests and preferences.

GENOA TRAVEL
Itinerary Planner

	Time	Activities
Day 7		

	Time	Activities
Day 8		

CONCLUSION

Wow! Can you believe we've reached the end of our journey through the beautiful city of Genoa? As we wrap up this guide penned by yours truly, Alec James, my hope is that this guide has served as your faithful companion and I want to take a moment to reflect on the incredible adventure we've had together.

From the moment I started writing these pages, I couldn't help but feel a rush of excitement – the same kind of excitement you get when you're about to set foot in a new, unknown place. I've poured my heart and soul into these words, hoping to convey the magic that Genoa holds within its cobblestone streets and historic palaces.

But here's the thing, my friend – a guide can only show you the way; it's up to you to create your own unique experience. I've shared my own stories and insights, but I can't wait to hear about the stories you'll write in the margins of these pages. The laughter shared in a quaint trattoria, the awe-inspired moments in front of centuries-old art, the serenity of watching the sun set over the Ligurian Sea – these are the moments that make your journey truly yours.

As you close this book, remember that Genoa is more than just a city; it's a feeling, an emotion that will stay with you long after you've returned home. And guess what? This isn't goodbye; it's more like "until we meet again." The well layered roads, the lively markets, the sea breeze - they'll be here when you come back, ready to welcome you with open arms.

So, my fellow adventurer, go forth and explore, seek out new horizons, and carry a piece of Genoa with you wherever you go. Share your experiences, swap stories, and keep the spirit of this incredible city alive in your heart. May your travels be filled with wonder, laughter, and the kind of moments that make you feel truly alive.

Safe Travels!

GENOA TRAVEL

Itinerary Planner

	Time	Activities
Day 9		

	Time	Activities
Day 10		

GENOA TRAVEL
Itinerary Planner

Day 11

Time	Activities

Day 12

Time	Activities

166

GENOA TRAVEL
Itinerary Planner

Time	Activities

Day 13

Time	Activities

Day 14

GENOA TRAVEL
Itinerary Planner

Time	Activities

Day 15

Time	Activities

Day 16

.

Printed in Great Britain
by Amazon

28659970R00097